MASTERS' MANUAL Of H'SING - I KUNG FU

By

John L. Price

Masters' Manual
of
H'sing-I Kung Fu

ISBN 978-1-4303-2831-5

Published by lulu.com

2nd Edition

First Printing

Disclaimer

Please note that the author and publisher of this instructional book are NOT RESPONSIBLE in any manner whatsoever for practicing the techniques or following any instruction given within this manuscript. Since the activities given here may be too strenuous for some readers, it is deemed ***Essential that you seek a doctor's permission to perform them.***

Dedication

I wish to thank Master Hsu for teaching and guiding me all these years. His patience and endurance had to be monumental to have taken on that job. Without him, this book would not have been written. In addition, thanks and appreciation must be given to all of the great masters of H'sing-I from the past, for without them this knowledge would not have been passed on to our generation.

Acknowledgments

I would like to thank my wife for her selfless work on this book. Without her typing and retyping the original manuscript, this book would never have seen the light of day.

Also, thanks to Roger West and Mori Thompson who edited and wrote the descriptions for all the photos.

I would like to thank all of the students who took part in the shooting of the pictures. I appreciate their time contributed to the making of this book.

Again, special thanks go out to my wife and my students Arlene DeFillipo and Jim Shoemaker, in the Redding area, who have unselfishly edited, critiqued and, in general, brought this publication to light again.

Table of Contents

Forward

2nd Edition

It has been 30 years this year since the Masters' Manual of H'sing-I Kung Fu was first published. I have decided to reprint it after receiving many inquires from martial artists throughout the country.

To my knowledge this was the first book ever printed in the English language to contain the inner knowledge of H'sing-I Kung Fu. The scope of the original was to introduce to the world the depth and boundless horizons of the Chinese Martial Arts. It did that and more. For three decades people have tried to obtain a copy of this book and now it will be available for a limited time again.

Preparing the book for reprinting has proven to be a difficult task. The original printing plates were destroyed in the late 90's. Without the original plates we have to use an existing book to reproduce the images for the edition. The quality will be somewhat lower, but wherever we are able, we will use the original pictures. I have made annotations where I feel they are needed to update the book.

For the 30th anniversary of the Masters' Manual we are including some of the herbal formulas that have worked for many for years. As a matter of fact, some of these formulas have been used for centuries.

In several areas of this second edition I have added extra content. You can identify the changes in the 2007 Edition by the italics.

I hope that you will enjoy reading and viewing the photos as much as I did preparing it for publication again.

John L. Price

In Memoriam

I met Master Hsu in March of 1967. He was the head assistant to Hung I Shung of the *Wu Tao Kwoon* Kung Fu School in Taipei, Taiwan. I, like everyone else who studied there, liked him immediately.

When he left Master Hung in July of 1967 and opened his own school most of the American students went with him. His English was much better than Master Hung's. From that beginning I followed Master Hsu until his death in 1984.

Following Master Hsu's teachings was at times very difficult. I had gone days without sleep on many occasions because he wanted to test my desire. He didn't always seem fair, but I quickly learned that life isn't fair, it is just life. He put martial arts into a daily living scenario. I failed many attempts by Master Hsu to educate me on the Chinese style of learning. It was extremely difficult at times for the learning because of the language barrier. I learned as much Chinese as I could and Master Hsu learned as much English as he could just to continue the teaching process.

Master Hsu lived with my family from June 1975 until February 1979. He would spend six months with us and six months in Taiwan. We became very close.

Master Hsu has been gone now for over 20 years and at times it is still difficult for me to believe he is truly gone. He was the most vibrant, upbeat personality I have ever met, and he will be very hard to replace. The 3 A.M. instruction sessions I used to take for granted are gone now, never to return. I have missed them.

(2007 edition)

Master Hsu Hong Chi

In 1934 in Taipei, Taiwan there was born a male child to the house of Hsu. This was a time for rejoicing and merriment. Little did anyone know that Hsu Hong Chi would later become the head of an International Kung Fu Association.

The young Hsu Hung Chi was one of six brothers, and like his siblings, he was a devoted and respectful son. With his older brothers, Hsu Hong Chi was taken to a Buddhist monk to have his future told. He was informed that he would one day be a leader of men. This knowledge was to stick with him all his life.

In his early school years, Hsu Hong Chi participated in many types of sports, excelling in swimming, soccer and judo. He was a natural athlete. The study of Kung Fu was initiated by his father. This was Shaolin and, unimpressed at his young age by martial arts, he chose to study western boxing instead.

Young Hsu Hong Chi did well in school, but he preferred to fight after school. He would rather fight than eat. On one momentous day when he was fourteen, he got into a fight that changed his life. The opponent was a country boy who had come to visit the city (Taipei). As often happens when two young people from opposite backgrounds meet, an argument and fight resulted. As Hsu opened his attack it was parried quite easily and two thrusts to his solar plexus were delivered.

Reacting from his experience he escaped injury, but realized his opponent's Kung Fu was far superior to his own style of street fighting. Experience won him the fight, and he began his study of Kung Fu soon after and never turned back.

Just as with every Chinese who is exposed to Martial Arts, Hsu Hong Chi formally began his training in Shaolin.

After years of many long days of practice, Master Hsu changed to H'sing-I Ch'uan. His study of H'sing-I was disrupted only once, by his tour of duty in the Air Force.

Not attending college, as his father had wanted, Hsu Hong Chi could expect no help from his family. Staying with Kung Fu was a very difficult choice for him to make.

That he did persevere and succeed is now history, and as his ability and love of H'sing-l grew, so did his following. With many Americans, Okinawans, Japanese and Chinese prodding him, he finally asked his teacher for permission to open his own school. In May 1967, the God Dragon H'sing-I Kwoon was opened.

By 1970 Shoufu Hsu was teaching at five universities. This was done with the aid of his senior students. In 1972, he was afforded a privilege rarely given to a Chinese. Hsu was given a special pass to an American military installation. This was Shou Lin Kou Air Station. Soon three more military classes were begun at C.C.K. Air Base, M.A.A.G. Compound, and Navy Compound.

In 1973, Shoufu Hsu formed the Tang Shou Tao (Way of China Hand) Kung Fu Association. This association has now grown into the International Tang Shou Tao Association with Japan, Kuwait, Philippines Italy, Germany, Mexico, R.O.C., Australia and the United States all as member countries.

In addition to his duties as head of his own association, Master Hsu was a special advisor to many other groups and associations, including the Bok Mei Kung Fu Association of Hong Kong and Japan Karate Federation. He also served as referee to the Taipei Athletic Association. Master Hsu's visits to the United States were a prelude to travels to his member countries. With his guidance and training, each of his students has prospered both physically and mentally.

About the Author

John L. Price was born in the United States and had little time in his youth to study any martial art, even if it had been available, which it wasn't. Growing up in the 1950's, on a farm in Louisiana, left no time for martial arts.

In 1966, John entered the U.S. Army and concluded training at Ft. Devens, Massachusetts in January of 1967. Upon completion, trainees were stationed around the world. John volunteered for radio direction finding school and an assignment to Vietnam. The school was cancelled and John was then assigned to Taiwan. He reported for duty to the Shu Lin Kou Air Station February of 1967.

Taiwan was a cultural shock, but a great assignment to receive. It was also the best-kept secret of the Army Security Agency. It was mostly for Vietnam vets or second term re-enlistees. John was the first new guy to be stationed there from the army in over ten years.

He took advantage of this and studied twice a day on his days off. It was with great sorrow that he left Taiwan in June 1970 to return to the United States. Upon finishing his army duty, he returned home to a civilian job and began to raise his family.

The first God Dragon, or Shen Lung, Kung Fu School in the United States was opened in April of 1973. That school was the first Tang Shou Tao School to open in the United States. In 1977, John Price became the first vice president of the International Tang Shou Tao Association and served until 1980.

Respect Is the Key

In centuries past and in part even today, the Chinese seeking instruction in the martial arts had to go through some sort of initiation to prove their willingness to learn and in ancient times was often refused by the great masters.

If the prospective student was considered he might be made to wait six months just to enter the master's house, thus testing his patience and desire to learn. If he passed this test and gained entrance, he was given menial tasks to test his patience and endurance further. If after this the master was satisfied, he would be instructed by one of the senior students. It was sometimes years before the master would personally instruct a new student. This style of seeking and obtaining instruction is in great contrast to the method of seeking instruction today.

Today, especially in the West, a student simply walks into a school, puts down his money and expects to be taught all of the teacher's knowledge.

When I began my study of Kung Fu in Taiwan I was from the same mold as any other American. I didn't realize how deep and involved Kung Fu truly is. There is this analogy: many people are like a blind man who, upon bumping into an elephant, shouted indignantly, "Why don't you watch where you are going!?" They can't see how large the elephant is and that it could easily crush them, though, in its benevolence, it continues on its way.

After many years of study from Master Hsu, he slowly opened my eyes and I began to see the profoundness of the art. I witnessed many episodes and incidents in my years in Taiwan.

One of the most memorable was when Master Hsu attempted instructing a student who persisted in saying "I know, I know." Finally the Master's words would not suffice; he instructed the student to punch, and after easily deflecting the punch he slapped the student innocently on his side, and walked away not saying a word. Three days later, at a friend's apartment, while watching TV, the student doubled over in pain clutching the spot slapped by Master Hsu. His friends rushed him to the Navy hospital but the doctors were unable to diagnose or relieve the pain permanently. Finally, another student notified Master Hsu and pleaded with him to come and help. Master Hsu went to the Navy hospital and, under the disbelieving eyes of the doctors, placed his hand under the covers, using an acupressure technique to completely relieve the pain. Later, this student was to become a senior student of the Master.

This incident, along with others, opened my eyes to the depth of Kung Fu and made me realize the importance of having the utmost respect when learning this art. This is overlooked probably 99% of the time by American students. Respect is basic to any learning and is given too little attention by most people.

Respect goes hand in hand with another concept which is called "ren," meaning "to endure". The combination of respect and ren is the way to learning Kung Fu. Most Americans seem to find these concepts difficult. A good illustration of "ren" is the time Master Hsu wished to test the heart of one Chinese student. This student had trimmed Master Hsu's finger nails and the Master's son had put the clippers away when Master Hsu mentioned that his toenails should also be trimmed. The student got up to get the clippers but the Master suggested that the student could bite them off with his teeth. The student, without hesitating, knelt at the Master's feet, took off his shoes and was about to begin when the Master pulled his foot away and told his student it was not necessary. Out of trust and devotion the student passed this test of the heart. Of course with this ability to endure, the teacher will teach his student anything. How many Americans would humble themselves enough to endure this kind of test? I would gamble, not many.

A person in a traditional Oriental society has a jump on the American in learning Kung Fu because the concepts of respect and ren have been ingrained in them since childhood and are further cultivated in the Kung Fu training. On the other hand, most American students do not realize the depth of Kung Fu or the importance of respect and ren, and therefore will lose this time to a person who already knows. I have been there and have experienced it.

We had asked Master Hsu to come to the U.S. and help us set up a school. To test our patience, he refused for five years. Finally in 1975, he consented to a visit. Anxious to give him a first-hand look at the Martial Arts in the United States, we tried to take him to visit many schools and showed him many American books on the subject. He always refused our invitations to visit other schools. Even while sitting in my home when I tried to get him to comment on various American publications, he would only say that they were good, and then put them aside.

Since I had opened my school in the States, all I had been used to hearing was that this style is better than that style, or this one is only for exercise, or that style is more powerful than another. All Master Hsu would say was that any style is good. This was quite different than what I was used to hearing. Finally, I had to confront him and ask why he would never comment on the books l had shown him. He exclaimed, "Why? I will tell you! Kung Fu, of course, is good. But you asked me to read and comment on the American Publications, so I will. Many people in this country study for a year or so at one style and then, feeling they have mastered it, switch to another school where they think they can learn more. They never stay with any one style long enough to master it or to form "Gan-H'sing" (heart and heart) with any one teacher."

Gan H'sing, or the bond of love and mutual respect that is formed between a teacher and a pupil, is the basis for true learning. It is only formed after years of the continuous dedication of a student to his teacher. This lack of Gan H'sing is evident by looking around and noticing how many students have studied from this teacher and that one. After changing teachers several times they end up with nothing, because if they were to need the help of a teacher, who would help them?

Americans with only five or six years of this kind of experience write books on Kung Fu. Most Chinese teachers of 20 or 30 years never write a book. Because of this poor method of learning, their books are filled with pictures of mistakes in forms and techniques.

Chinese Kung Fu teachers look at these publications and laugh inside but make no comment outright. The secrets of Kung Fu are still secure with them.

After listening to Master Hsu's explanation, I felt uneasy because secretly I had wanted to write a book. So instead, I asked Master Hsu if I could write a book for him in order that some of his knowledge may be imparted to the American public. He consented and the next two years were spent in compiling information and translating from Chinese to English the material in this book.

Kung Fu: A Short History

Kung Fu is indigenous to China. It is agreed on by most historians to be approximately 4,500 years old. The term "Kung Fu" by itself means the ability to do a job and alone does not refer to the martial arts. The correct term and the one which is most often used in China is "Wu Shu." However the term "Kung Fu" will be used in this book in referring to the martial arts so as not to create confusion and because we have become accustomed to hearing it applied in that manner in the West.

The history of martial arts in China is long and somewhat obscure. There are many different theories, which account for the origin and lineage of Kung Fu and historians have not always been able to agree on any particular explanation.

Undoubtedly, when dealing with the past, facts and legends may become intertwined and the job of sorting out the whole truth becomes near impossible or at least very complex. The task becomes more difficult the further back in time one goes. So, to account for nearly 5,000 years of Kung Fu history would take a great deal of time and effort. That task can be handled infinitely better by those more qualified than myself. This book will not deal in any great detail with the history of martial arts since it is not within the scope or purpose of this publication. I would merely like to present a general overview of the subject so that the reader may have some basic idea of Kung Fu before delving into the heart of this book, which is H'sing-I.

There are over 365 different styles. Out of all these styles, which are still practiced in China and abroad, there are in reality only two main divisions. One is the Shaolin style, which is of the Buddhist school of thought. Buddhism originated in India and spread to China. The other is the Wu Tang style that is of Taoist origin, a philosophy which is native to China, and one which was practiced before the arrival of Buddhism.

Under the heading of Shaolin Kung Fu, there are well over 360 styles. Shaolin Kung Fu developed from various fighting techniques that had already evolved in China. Within these temples the martial arts were cultivated and refined. The essence of the Shaolin style is the 18 hand techniques. Bodhiharma, the 20th patriarch of Buddhism, introduced the Chan, or Zen in Japanese, aspect of this philosophy to China. Chan is the art of health nourishing. This addition increased the popularity of the already famous Shaolin Temple.

Chinese history celebrates Ch'an San Fung, a Taoist born during the Ming Dynasty, as the founder of the soft school Wu Tang. Unlike the Shaolin styles, the Tao styles did not place great importance on physical strength. Through the practice of this soft style, they hoped to relieve tension and stress on the internal organs and promote a healthy body.

Through diligent practice, the internal art of the soft styles helps to soothe the nervous system, produce internal heat, regulate the transition from old to new and regenerate the function of the degenerated internal organs. The spiritual aspect of doing nothing and yet getting everything done was instilled in the Wu Tang School. The internal styles were still linked to the Shaolin styles because most students or Kung Fu began their training with Shaolin and progressed to Wu Tang.

H'sing-I Ch'uan: An Explanation

H'sing-l Ch'uan (pronounced shing-ee-chen) is an internal form of boxing. Along with Tai Chi Ch'uan and Pa Kua Ch'uan, they make up the three internal styles of the Wu Tang School. General Yueh Fei (岳飛) is usually credited as the founder of H'sing-I.

H'sing-I (**形意 拳**) has been translated into various western terms: *form-will, body-mind* or simply *mind-boxing*. Each of these suggests the interaction of the mind and body as an integral principle of this style. However, what they are missing is the essence of the concept, the interaction of body and mind.

This concept is easier to understand by translating H'sing-I as heart and mind, the heart being the seat of emotions, controlling the body and responsible for its reactions. Therefore, the word "H'sing" should not be translated literally as *form* or simply *body*, because in referring to this style the concept of the heart is more accurate.

The word *I* translates as *mind*, but includes the meaning of *will*. The overall meaning then is the bringing of the heart and mind into harmony. In practical terms, if you have ever been struck at and had to react quickly you may know of what I am speaking.

When you practice the martial arts, you practice techniques of self-defense. These techniques become second nature because your mind has become unconscious of the moves. Quite often though, when you react to an attack, there is a hesitation. This is because your heart is fearful and wants to be overly cautious. This hesitation can be fatal because a split second can determine your victory or defeat.

In essence, your mind and heart are not in balance. To bring about harmony is the purpose of H'sing-I Ch'uan. The most important point to learn when you start practicing H'sing-l

Ch'uan is to relax. Relax the mind as well as the body and then the movements become smooth and natural. H'sing-I does not make use of an external imaginary opponent in the performance of its sets (katas). The mind is turned inwards, concentrating on the movements and the breath.

As you begin to progress, you will speed up when you do the sets. Speed though is not the goal here either, spontaneity is. All your reactions must become relaxed and natural. Ultimately your mind moves your body. This is not easy to understand or obtain. Years of practice and patience, combined with a good teacher can get you there. In solo practice your objective is harmony in your actions.

In terms of the hard and soft styles, even true Shaolin is soft. When people look at Shaolin what they perceive is a mistake. They see the speed within the movement. They perceive that the speed is delivered with great power throughout the movement, but in actuality the force is applied at the moment of contact; on the other hand, just as important as punching is how you receive the force of your opponents attack and how you counter. You must learn how to suck him in, raise him, swallow him and lower him. You do not oppose hard with hard. You counter hard with soft and strike with a shock punch. (1) The secret of the shock punch is in the waist and shoulders. Properly done they can fatally injure a man. The force of your opponent's attack is linked with your own counter to create a circle helping to use the attacker's own force against himself. This circle is very dangerous and can only be taught to a student after he has obtained a great degree of cultivation of his heart which is the essence of Chinese Kung fu.

To get someone down cleverly though is not the most important thing. The first rule is to have respect for your opponent.

(1) Shock punch: As the name implies, this is the method of punching which delivers a great shock to the opponent. The shock is generated by a stomping motion of the foot at the moment the punch contacts the opponent.

The Unique Chi of H'sing-I Ch'uan & The Wu H'sing Ch'uan

The universe was originally in chaos, amorphous and senseless, whereas before it was contained by "chi" (2). Then the chi flowed into every corner of the universe and life was thus generated. This is called the "Unique Chi", or as some say "Congenital true chi".

As the chi induced the "Lian leh" (3), the sky and earth were separated, "Yin and Yang" (4) were distinguished, and man emerged.

Therefore chi is the root of all life, the spring of faith and the bases of immortality. It is through the process of chi that men are alive. Maintaining it, life is prolonged; spoiling and scattering it, life is doomed. H'sing-I Ch'uan utilizes a system of exercises for the human body to harmonize "Yin and Yang," to adapt with faith, to exchange "Chien and Kuen" (5), to shift the "acquired ability into the congenital power," and eventually maintaining chi to the utmost of life!

Hence, Kung fu may be complicated and diverse, but generally speaking, it is no more than "exercising chi".

Induced by the "Unique Chi", "Lian leh" is the sky and earth, and also "Yang and Yin".

Yang . . . . Masculine

Yin . . . . .Feminine

Alone, neither Yin nor Yang can form life; it is nature's rule that the two together generate life.

(2) Life force (3) Sky and earth (4) Yang = masculine, sun/ Yin = feminine, moon (5) Chien--masculine element as represented in the I Ching by 3 solid lines. Kuen is the feminine element represented by 3 broken lines.

The human body can be thought of as a miniature universe, with any limb or bone or a single gesture categorized by being either Yin or Yang. When the two are harmonized the body is strong and movement strong. When the two are violated, the body is weak and movement bewildered. Since Yin and Yang come from the "Congenital True Chi," the only way to maintain this "Unique Chi" is to start from harmonizing Yin and Yang. This is the reason anyone practicing H'sing-I Ch'uan must understand Lian leh.

Wu H'sing is the heart of H'sing-I Ch'uan. Wu H'sing means 5 forms or styles (Gold, Wood, Water, Fire and Soil.) There is a relation between Wu H'sing and life. The inner and outer 5 essential organs of the body are all classified according to Wu H'sing respectively.

	GOLD	WATER	WOOD	FIRE	SOIL
Inner 5 Organs	Lung	Kidney	Liver	Heart	Spleen
Outer 5 organs	Nose	Ears	Eyes	Tongue	Mouth

Each of the 5 elements has specific strengthening and restraining powers on the others. See figure 1.

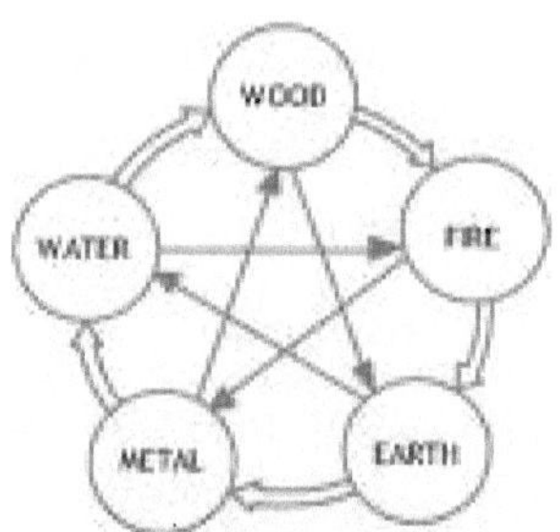

Outer circle creates / Inner lines control

Figure 1

Practicing Wu H'sing- I will bring about the Yin/Yang balance in your body.

External Body:	Shoulder	Yang
	Pelvis	Yin
	Elbow	Yang
	Knee	Yin
	Hand	Yang
	Foot	Yin
	Harmony	
External Movement	Stretch	Yang
	Bend	Yin
	Again	Harmony
	Up	Yang
	Down	Yin

Furthermore, Yin may exist in Yang, and the latter in the former. Yin at its highest level may give rise to Yang, and vice versa. Only under the most thorough observations can one distinguish the complex differences between the two.

The five styles of Ch'uan (fist) are also classified in terms of how the chi moves or are moved according to the 5 actions as follows:

	NAME	FORM	ELEMENT	ORGAN
1.	**Pi Ch'uan**	**Ax**	**Metal**	**Lung**

The power of Ch'uan is natural. The chi of the lungs is smooth, which also makes the body strong.

2.	**Tsuan Ch'uan**	**Lightening**	**Water**	**Kidney**

Chi flow is complete. Chi is smooth and the kidneys will be healthy. The clear chi rises and the bad chi lowers.

3.	**Peng Ch'uan**	**Arrow**	**Wood**	**Liver**

Chi stretches in and out. The liver is stabilized and the spirit is induced. The muscles and bones will be strong and the brain can be shrewd.

4.	**Pao Ch'uan**	**Cannon**	**Fire**	**Heart**

Chi opens as if a cannon fires. The heart is widened and the body is comfortable.

5.	**Heng Ch'uan**	**Marbles**	**Earth**	**Stomach**

The union of the chi. the shape is round, the nature is solid. The Wu H'sing is harmonized and life generated.

Again, as in figure 1, the Wu H'sing has the same strengthening and weakening powers on each other. A person who practices will undergo certain changes in his or her body. The following is a chart of those changes:

First: The Three Principles of H'sing-I Ch'uan.

A. Refine "Ching"(6) to chi.

B. Refine "Chi" to "Shen". (7)

C. Refine Shen back to Emptiness. (8)

Second: Three Major Steps in H'sing-I Ch'uan.

A. Modify Bone

B. Modify Muscle

C. Modify the Spinal Cord

Third: Three Ways in which to practice H'sing-I Ch'uan.

1. Visible Strength

2. Invisible Strength

3. Refined Inner Strength

These are the principles and steps to return to a younger condition in your mind and body. The Chinese believe that a baby's mind is like a tape with nothing on it. After all your years of problems and troubles, your ideas and mind are cluttered. So, to return to this clean slate of mind is the objective of H'sing-I Ch'uan. It goes almost without saying that children heal faster, are more flexible, and generally better fit. If you could return to this condition you would be more physically and mentally alert and have a long life.

(6) Seminal Essence (7) Spiritual Essence (8) Back to before birth.

Overall Essence of H'sing-I

In order to practice this art to the fullest one must be familiar with the principles behind the many techniques and forms. Following is a list of the basic principles underlying this style. This list presents the overall essence of H'sing-I Ch'uan. No attempt to explain these principles is made because to understand these principles intellectually is useless. However, if you practice H'sing-I these principles can be applied in a practical sense. The longer one practices, the clearer these principles will become and with each unveiling greater progress is made. Again let me state that these principles will become clearer the more one considers them and practices.

3 UPTHRUSTS

Up thrust your head as if up thrusting the roof.

Up thrust your tongue to the palate.

Up thrust your palms upward as if upholding objects.

"Understanding the '3 UPTHRUSTS', strength is built to lift trees."

3 SUPPRESSES

Suppress downward your chin, but to gaze straight forward.

Suppress your hands with upper arms, but to be natural.

Suppress your feet with waist and back, but to be closely linked.

"Understanding the '3 SUPPRESSES', spirit and mind is induced."

3 CURVES

Curve shoulders and back to be a hemisphere.

Chest curved, "Chi" is broadened.

"Hu Kou" (between thumb and index finger) to be curved as crescent moon.

"Understanding the '3 Curves', the secret is unveiled."

3 EMBRACES

"Tan Tien" (hypogastrium) to be embraced with "Chi" as the root.

Heart to be embraced with body as the basis.

Arm to be embraced with four limbs firmly still.

Understanding the '3 EMBRACES', body is guarded.

3 SINKS

With "Chi" sunk in Tan Tien, illness is excluded.

With upper arm sinking downward, deep meaning there hidden.

With elbows sinking downward, shoulders are the roots.

"Understanding the '3 SINKS', body is keen and shrewd."

3 CRESCENT MOONS

Arms as bows like the crescent moon.

Wrists thrusting outward like the crescent moon.

Legs and knees bent like the crescent moon.

Understanding the "3 Crescent Moons", posture is best oriented.

3 STOPS (steadiness)

Neck shortened and upward-stopping, body is up straight.

Body stop on 4 sides.

Legs and knees downward stopping, as roots of trees.

"Understanding the "3 Stops", Kung fu is well rooted.

2007

2nd Edition

More explanation is given to the cryptic verse provided in the original book.

1. *3 Up thrusts: Strength comes from uniting the mind and body.*
2. *3 Suppresses: Opens the gates on the spine to allow the chi to ascend.*
3. *3 Curves: The chi circulation is completed.*
4. *3 Embraces: Prevents illness.*
5. *3 Sinks: The mind and body are ready and centered.*
6. *3 Crescent Moons: Makes the use of the energy more efficient.*
7. *3 Stops: This is in reference to the bodies being rooted to the ground.*

Important Means

When my wife and I began training in H'sing-I Ch'uan, we had no idea what we were in for. I was young and thought I was strong. After one day I knew I was not as strong as I had believed. After the general exercises, we started our practice with Pi Ch'uan (Ax or Metal). In less than two minutes my legs would shake so badly I was embarrassed at my lack of endurance. In performing the Pi Ch'uan posture the majority of the weight is carried by the rear leg, the front foot lightly touching the ground. If I had too much weight on the front legs when the assistant would sweep them, I would fall down. Shoufu would only say, "One more time."

Many months passed and my Pi Ch'uan finally improved. This is only the first style (element). All five forms of Wu H'sing require months of practice to achieve an intermediate proficiency. What this teaches a person is difficult to understand. Practicing daily brought about certain ideas and procedures. I could not explain all of them because at the time I did not know them. Master Hsu started explaining about the principles of H'sing-I Ch'uan. Everything I had studied was explained, only I had not known the theories and principles. When Master Hsu had agreed to write this book, he also gave some of the principles and theories. One of the first set of rules is called the "Combination of Six" (Lieo Ho)

1. The six styles of the body are:

A. Chicken legs	B. Dragon trunk	C. Bear shoulders
D. Eagle claws	E. Tigers embrace	F. Thunder & Roaring

2. Combination of Six--Lieo Ho:

A. Inner Combination of 3	B. Outer Combination of 3
Heart—Mind	Hands--Feet
Mind--Chi	Elbow--Knee
Chi—Strength	Shoulders--"Kua" (hip)

This combination of six is then used with the "Seven Stars." These are: hand, foot, head, elbow, knee, "Kua" (hip), and shoulder. These are the weapons of the human body that can attack with fatal power.

After these rules comes the means by which you can successfully deliver your attack. They are as follows:

1. To strike is to be "all out". To move hands and legs together. Fists as cannons, body as a dragon. Move as if you have flames all over the body in the face of an attacker.

2. Head hit. The whole body moves as one. The feet take position in center.

3. Shoulder hit. One is Yin (back) and one is Yang (front). Hands are hidden. Right or left depends on the situation.

4. Hand hit. Moving from your chest it is like a tiger catching a lamb. Strength put in hands should be instantly variable. Elbows are to be lower than armpits.

5. Kua hit. Yin or Yang, left or right is up to the situation. Be natural while moving feet. Be quick as a sword while attacking.

6. Knee hit. Strike on vital points can be fatal. Hands up balancing the body.

7. Feet hit. Steps are firm. The strength comes from foot rooted to the ground; never let your attempt be known. Power of a tornado.

5 Elements Pictorial

1. PI CH'UAN

To begin, start with your feet together, left toes pointing straight ahead, the right toes at a 45 degree angle to the right and heels touching. Right hand on left, palms up with tips of thumbs touching, eyes looking ahead. Tongue is against the pallet (Photo 1-1).

Photo 1-1

Next, the hands are raised in an arc to the side, palms up, as you inhale. On reaching the highest point above the head, the hands come together with thumbs and index fingers touching (Photo 1-2).

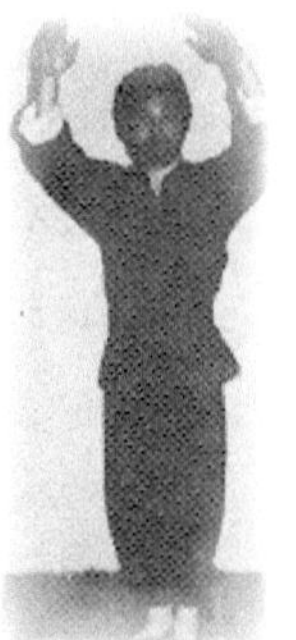

Photo 1-2

The hands are then lowered together down the center of the body to just below the navel as you exhale. The knees bend slightly as the hands are lowered, palms down (Photo 1-3).

Photo 1-3

From this point the hands turn up while making fists. The right fist, palm up, punches out and up to nose level (Photo 1-4). The left fist rests, palm up, in the bend of the right elbow. The weight is shifted to the right foot with the left foot lightly touching the ground with the ball of the foot.

Photo 1-4

This is all executed in one movement. The hands then open as the right hand drops in an arc to the level of the navel, palm down and the left strikes forward in an arc with finger tips at nose level as the left hand strikes forward the left foot steps forward and the right foot slides forward slightly to maintain balance. This is called a half-step and plays a very important role in H'sing-I (Photo 1-5).

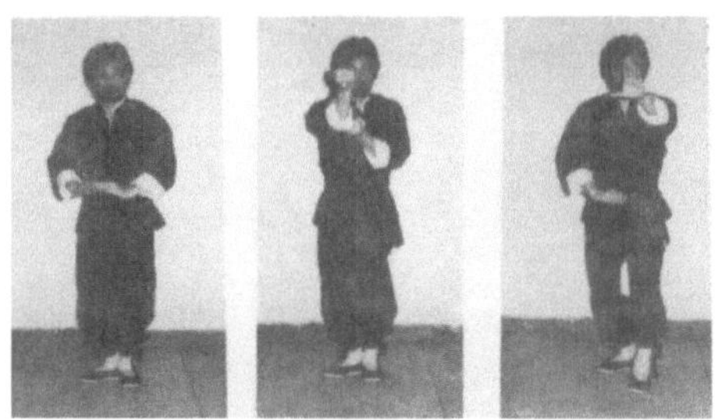

Photo 1-5

2. TSUAN CH'UAN

Begin with the Pi Ch'uan posture, left hand up, right hand down. Left hand twists, palm up, fingers come together here as the left foot slides forward, carrying the majority of the weight with the toe pointing out to a 45 degree angle. The left elbow, knee, and ankle should be vertically lined up. The left hand makes a fist as the right hand and foot come forward in unison. The right hand is in a fist and punches out and up to nose level while left is brought down in front of the navel. The raising right hand follows a path inside that of the dropping left. The left hand is then in a fist, palm down. The right foot has stepped through to a forward position and the left follows in a sliding half-step as in Pi Ch'uan. At this point the same process is repeated beginning on the right (Photo 2-1, 2-2, and 2-3).

Photo 2-1

Photo 2-2

Photo 2-3

3. **PENG CH'UAN**

Begin with the Pi ch'uan posture left hand and foot forward. From this position the right hand makes a fist, raises approximately to the solar plexus and punches straight out and slightly down. In its course, the right fist and wrist brush over the left hand, this drops and is pulled back to the waist as a fist. As the right hand punches, the right foot slides forward level with the left stopping with an audible stomp. Next, the left fist punches, first coming to the center of the body in front of the solar plexus, brushing over the right arm which is drawn back to the waist. In this step the left foot steps out and the right follows with a sliding half-step, though not coming to an even position with the right. Since we began with the left foot leading in step 1, it will continue to lead, the right foot should not pass the left. (Photos 3-1, 3-2, and 3-3)

Photo 3-1

Photo 3-2

Photo 3-3

When punching with the right hand, the right foot comes to an even position with the left. This is called a "closed" position. When the left hand punches, the left foot is forward and the right foot takes only a half-step. Begin with right hand and foot forward in Pi Ch'uan, then the right foot will continue to lead.

4. **PAO CH'UAN**

Begin in Pi Ch'uan posture, right hand and foot steps out and forward. Left foot steps out and forward at a 45 degree angle to the left. The right foot follows, stopping next to the left with only the ball of the foot and toes touching the ground lightly, this puts the majority of the weight on the left foot. As you are stepping, the hands close to make fists and drop with the forearms crossing in front of your body. As you reach the position with your weight on your left foot the hands are drawn from in front of your body to your sides at the waist. Fists should be palm up. From this point the right fist comes to the center of the body and then blocks up and over the head as the left hand comes to the center of the body and punches straight out at chest level. The right foot steps out at a 45 degree angle to the right as the left foot follows in a half step. All the moves in each step are carried out in unison with hand and feet coordinated together so that the body moves as a unit. From this position the right foot steps directly forward with the left foot following and stopping next to the right foot with only the toes and ball of the foot resting lightly on the ground. The majority of the weight should be on the right foot. The hand movements are identical, only the movements are reversed from left to right and right to left. (Photos 4-1 and 4-2) Continue in this manner, alternating from left to right and from right to left

Photo 4-1 Photo 4-2

5. **HENG CH'UAN**

Begin in Pi Ch'uan posture as in element four, Pao Ch'uan. The footwork in Heng Ch'uan is identical to that of Pao Ch'uan, so begin by stepping out to the left with the left foot at a 45 degree angle, as the right foot follows and rests lightly next to the left, the right hand closes to make a fist and turns palm up and left hand remains palm down and closing to make a fist. Again, remember that the body moves as a unit. From this position the right foot steps out and the left foot follows in a half-step. At the same time the left hand punches out and up to nose level, twisting its palm up at the last second. In its course, the back of the left fist rubs the underside of the right forearm beginning contact at the elbow. As the right fist drops to the navel it twists to face palm dawn. At this point, as in Pao Ch'uan, the right foot steps slightly forward as the left foot follows, resting lightly on the ball and toes next to the right. The hands move as in step 1, exchanging in the same manner (Photos 5-1 and 5-2).

Photo 5-1 Photo 5-2

Quite often in Kung fu the Master will write the actions of his art into rhyme or poetry. Master Hsu has provided the Five Elements according to their actions. They have been translated into English on the following pages.

PI CH'UAN

From the mouth, come the two fists closely held.
Up to the eyebrow, tsuans (9) the fore-fist.
Close behind the fore-fist, follows the hind fist.
Together with the crossing arm, the heart unites.
"Chi" falls to "Tan Tien"(10) as body moves.
Hind foot forward as the arms separate.
In a hemisphere "Hu Kou" opens while all fingers apart.
Fore-hand pushes to between the eyebrow and heart.
Under the armpit, the hind-hand stays.
Hand, nose, foot form the "3 point set".(11)
So, as Pi Ch'uan tsuans upward.
To the eyebrow, turned up the little finger.
Together sink the feet and hands, up thrust the tongue.
Advancing, changing styles, hind-palm sinks down.

(9) Tsuan: to thrust and twist. (10) Tan Tien: Hypogastrium. (11) 3 point set: Tip of hand, nose and foot in a line.

TSUAN CH'UAN

Fore-hand "Yin palm"(12) presses down.
Hind-hand "Yang fist"(13)upward tsuans.
Up to the eyebrows the fists tsuan,
Elbows embrace the heart while hind-foot moves.
Stare at fore-fist, four limbs stop.
Tsuan Ch'uan moves and styles changed.
Fore-foot steps first, hind-foot next,
Hind hand "Yin palm" down the elbows kept.
Step by step the 3 points set,
Fore-hand "Yang fist" hit the nose.
Little finger upward turned, heart by elbows protected.
Tsuan Ch'uan punches nose when advancing.
Fore-palm downward pressed with wrist,
Then upward turned as steps forward.

(12) Yin palm: palm facing downward. (13) Yang fist: fist with palm facing upward.

PENG CH'UAN

Peng Ch'uan starts with 3 points set.
"Hu Yen"(14) upward high as heart.
Hind-hand "Yang fist" under armpit stays,
Fore-foot forward, hind-foot next.
Shapes like "T", the two feet are firm,
Body turns while looking straight.
Up-straight standing when foot lift,
Lifted foot with toes pointing side-wise.
Hands and feet came down swiftly at same pace,
Fore-foot crossed then hind-one follows naturally.
Peng Ch'uan still has tongue at palate.
Fore-arms elbow curved to up thrust.
Punch to the armpits when advancing.
Be quick and firm, the hind-foot follows.

(14) Hu Yen: The Hu Kou position of a fist.

PAO CH'UAN

Elbows tightly embracing the body as foot lifted,
Fists in Yang fist must be tight.
Fore-hand be cross hind-hand, "T".(15)
Fists first stay beside the navel.
"Chi" falls to Tan Tien as style changes,
Keep the 3 paint set in place.
Fist outward, high as heart,
Fore-fists "Hu Yen" upward whi1e
Hind-fist tsuans up to eyebrows with
"Hu Yen" downwards and elbows too.
Pao Ch'uan must have foot lifted up.
Fore-fist tsuans up as foot drops.
"Crossing Steps" as fist and foot sink together
Thus follows the hind-foot on.

(15) "T" forming a shape of "T".

HENG CH'UAN

Fore-hand "Yang-fist", hind fist "Yin",
Hind-hand just below the elbow keeps.
Foot lifts up as fists move,
Body be firm and "Chi" is eased.
Tongue curls up and air exhales,
Feet close as scissors when style changes.
Half turn the body while foot-hand moves,
Hind-hand twists up and thrusts out.
Steps down, fists "Yang" and 3 points set,
Nose and feet is specially linked.
Heng Ch'uan always keep hind fist "Yin".
Fare-hand "Yang fist," elbows protects heart.
Left and right arms thrust out as bows.
Feet-hand sink together with tongue curled.

5 Elements Linked

In the following sequence, rather than show how Pi conquers Peng or number 5 succumbs to number 3, we have used prearranged sets. This is a two-man set that can go on as long as the two desire. It is a simple drill to teach the variations on the regular "5 Elements". It forms a circle or linked form "Lian Hwan".

Photo 6-1

I take the offensive and Master Hsu demonstrates the defense. I attack with a straight punch. Master Hsu steps outside of my attack with his left foot. Left hand blocks my punch (Photo 6-1).

Photo 6-2

This quickly changes into Pi Ch'uan (Photo 6-2).

To allow the reader a clearer picture of the counter to Master Hsu's Pi Ch'uan the next picture is reversed.

While I strike forward with Pi, Master Hsu quickly twists into Pao Chaun. (Photo 6-3) Then, just as quickly, Pao Ch'uan is dispatched by Tsuan Ch'uan

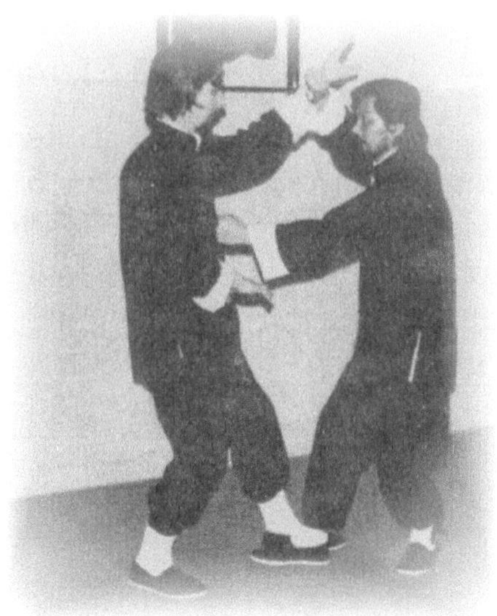

Photo 6-3

As the right hand rises in Pao Ch'uan (Photo 6-3), Master Hsu quickly pulls it downward and the right hand delivers an uppercut (Photo 6-4).

Photo 6-4

Photo 6-5

In (Photo 6-5), as my uppercut closes, it is picked off by a twisting forearm block, with the left arm.

Photo 6-6

The right arm now twists up and under the left to turn me further off center with my uppercut.

(Photo 6-6)

Common Mistakes

There are numerous publications devoted to the practice of the martial arts. These books, not unlike this one, are designed to aid the practitioner in increasing his knowledge and in instructing him "how to" perform sets and exercises. However, books that show the student what not to do are few and far between.

It is inevitable that when learning something new the beginner will make mistakes. This is a matter of course. The purpose of this next section is to demonstrate some of the most common mistakes made by beginners in an effort to preserve, as much as possible, the true art.

Each move has a meaning and each position held has been preserved through time for a specific purpose. Whether or not the student can comprehend this depends on the quality of his instruction and length of time he has studied. To modify an art which has stood the test of time (nearly 1,000 years) takes a person with a great ego, because he is making the assumption that by modifying a position or movement he is improving it. How can a man, in one lifetime, presume to be able to improve an art that has been conserved century upon century? It would require quite an exceptional individual to be able to modify or improve such an ancient art. Men of this stature are spaced sparsely throughout history. Yet, those who claim to improve an art through modification are numerous.

The mistakes shown in the following photos are a result of the violation of certain basic principles.

Photo 7-1

In (photo 7-1), the mistake is that I am leaning too far forward, which weakens my stance and causes imbalance. The principle violated here is that one's elbow should never extend past the knee.

Photo 7-2

(photo 7-2) Shows the correct posture with the elbow directly over the knee. This keeps the balance and allows me to move in any direction.

In (Photo 8-1), the student is tense and his shoulders are up. Because of this Chi is scattered and his heart is not comfortable. His movements will lack power.

Photo 8-1

In (photo 8-2), the student has corrected his position and relaxed his shoulders. This will allow him to improve his earth root and gain immense stability. The power that can be generated from the proper form is truly awesome.

Photo 8-2

Photo 9-1

In (photo 9-1), the student has not gauged the distance between herself and her opponent correctly. In delivering an attack, her effort is feeble and lacks power. Her elbows are extended past her knees and her shoulder is not over her hips.

Photo 9-2

In (photo 9-2), the position is corrected and the proper power may be delivered.

When blocking an attack it is a mistake to watch the opponent's hands. In (photo 10-1), the defender is leaving herself open and vulnerable to a follow-up attack by her enemy. By keeping her eyes on his hands she has not judged her distance properly.

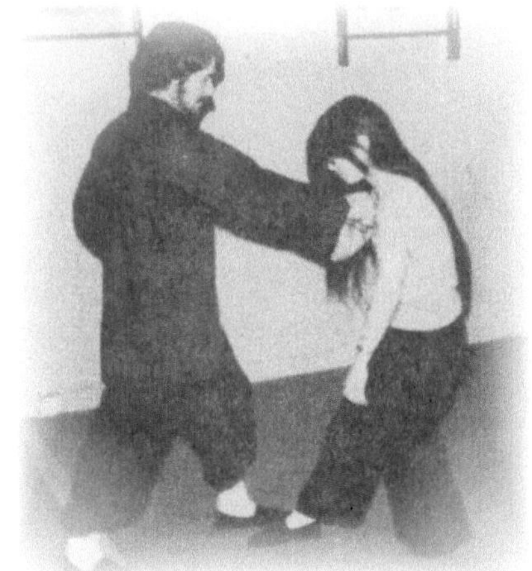

Photo 10-1

In (photo 10-2), by keeping her head up and facing her opponent she can take in a view of his whole body. One should not focus directly on a particular part of their opponent's body, but should try to keep a general view of their entire body.

Photo 10-2

These are a few of the common mistakes and violations of the basic principles as were taught to me by my teacher and as I teach them to my students.

Refer to the previous chapter on the principles of H'sing-I for details. Not only do these principles apply to H'sing-I, but to all styles of Kung Fu. All Kung Fu is the same in a final analysis.

The watchword is balance. This takes you all the way back to the Yin/Yang principles. When you either defend or attack, you must maintain your balance. This includes front-rear, left-right, and up-down. If you can keep your balance and disrupt your opponent you can emerge victorious.

The 12 Animals

In addition to the Wu H'sing five elements, there are the 12 animals which refer to the sets in this system. The Wu H'sing forms the basis and core of H'sing-I Ch'uan. The twelve animals are complimentary and enhance the five elements. With the five elements and the 12 animals, a student of H'sing-I has a wealth of techniques and variations from which he may choose the particular moves that suit his body type and stature.

In accordance with the principles of the Wu H'sing, it is true that all the techniques needed to deal with any situation are contained within the five elements. Thus, the five elements are the center of this style and the multitude of techniques that are generated by them. The 12 animal sets offer different techniques for the different types of people that practice this style. The twelve animals used in this style are:

1. Dragon:
2. Swallow
3. Snake
4. Chicken
5. Tortoise
6. Tiger
7. Phoenix
8. Sparrow-Hawk
9. Horse
10. Fighting Cock
11. Eagle-Bear
12. Monkey

Photo 11-1

In the following section we demonstrate a few of the techniques from the 12 animals. The techniques do not necessarily look like the animal that it represents, but they utilize the essence of that animal.

In (photos 11-1), the attacker strikes to the head. The defender deflects the punch…

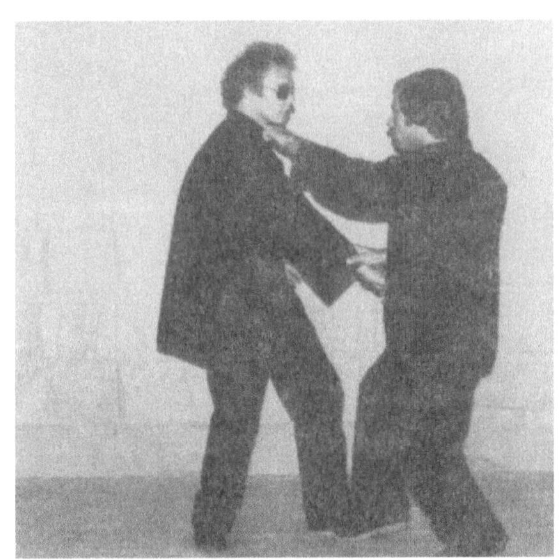

Photo 11-2

…and guides it down as he strikes up to the throat with his left. (photo 11-2). This technique is from the Chicken set.

(Photos 12-1 and 12-2) are also a variation of the Chicken style.

Both students begin with the san ti posture.

Photo 12-1

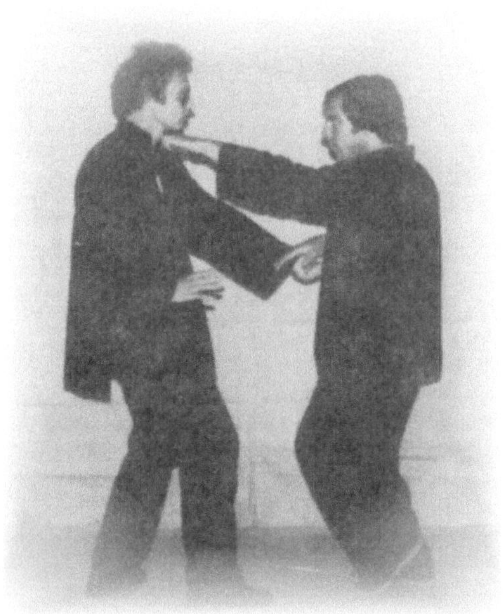

Photo 12-2

Using a technique from the Dragon style in Photo 13-1 I block my opponent's punch to mid-section with a circling motion. While I still control his hand, I strike to the head and kick the knee simultaneously (Photos 13-2 and 13-3).

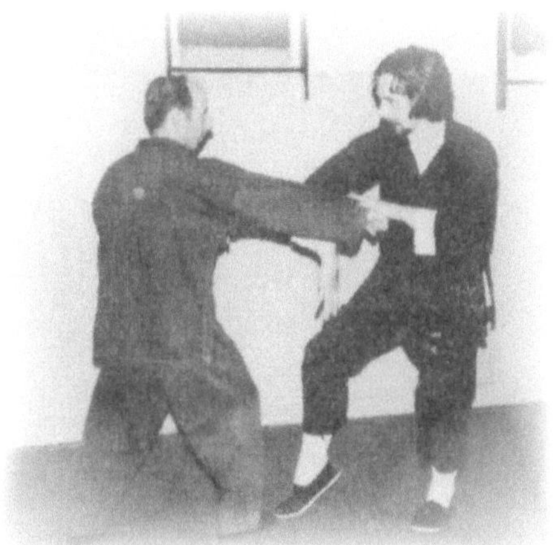

Photo 13-1

Photo 13-2

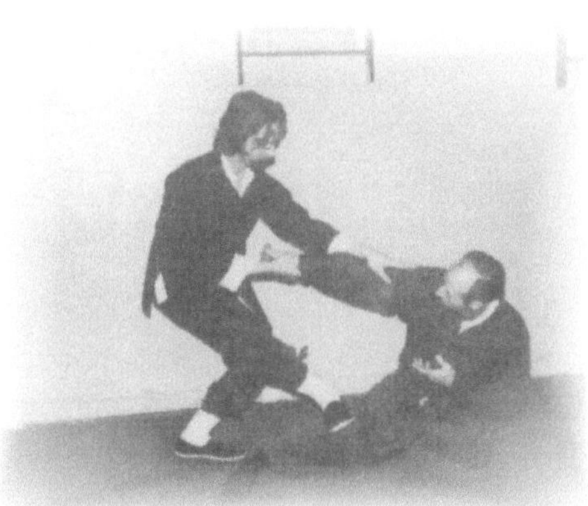

Photo 13-3

In Photo 14-1, the punch is blocked with the right and then caught with a twisting motion.

Photo 14-1

Following through to counter by rolling the edge of the hand and forearm along the back of the attackers elbow which in photos 14-2 and 14-3 could be easily broken. This technique is from the Snake set.

Photo 14-2

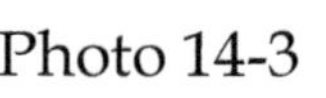

Photo 14-3

Photo 15-1

In the following techniques, the punch to the midsection is blocked with the right hand (Photo 15-1).

Photo 15-2

While at the same time, side step to the left, controlling the right hand, twist and kick to the small of the back. This side step and kick must be performed with split second timing or the move can be cutoff.

(Photo 15-2)

In the next sequence a right punch to the head is thrown. Again, a slight side step is used while simultaneously blocking with the left hand. (Photo 16-1)

Photo 16-1

In (Photo 16-2) we show the reverse side of the previous picture.

This shows the strike to the mid-section of the opponent.

Photo 16-2

These are but a few of the myriad techniques that are available in H'sing-I. These are neither the simplest nor the most difficult to perform. If you performed any technique, you would find that they all adhere to the principles set forth in the previous chapter. In my experience people use the techniques they like best, which is the most simple more often than not. In order to do these techniques, the body has an overall essence to which H'sing-I subscribes. We call them the "Nine Essences".

The Nine Essences

1. Body: Never can be powerful leaning forward, backward, to left or to right.

2. Shoulders: Head straight; shoulder drooping downward. Let your two shoulders move along with each other. It is through your shoulders that the strength in your body is transferred to your hands.

3. Arms: Left arm stretched forward, right arm close to your ribs. Be bent but not flexed, stretched but not straight. Too flexed never can reach far, too straight never can be powerful.

4. Hands: Right hand to armpit, left hand up to chest. The latter relaxed, the former strengthened. Hands both palm-side downward. Strength be even.

5. Fingers: Each separated, shape as hook, "Hu Kou" rounded, be hard and tender. Strength is to be at fingers but never forced.

6. Legs: Left to the front; right holding at back. Be straight but not, be bow but straight, straight or bow as a chicken.

7. Feet: All toes pointing forward, never to sides. Right back foot tends to be 45 degree sideward, following the ankle of foreleg. Distance is up to individual. Toes are firm.

8. Tongue: "Chi" will be weak if tongue is not rolled. Tan Tien lowered if eyes staring, hair standing, muscle on face be iron and inner organs are hardened.

9. Hips: Be tilted a little bit up so that "Chi" can be transferred to limbs, or else it will be scattered.

The Nine Essences

2007 Edition

The Essences are again referring to the correct body alignment. In the first addition of the Masters Manual, no explanation was given as Master Hsu thought that it would be better to let a person discover the results of his or her practice. The idea is to not give anyone a preconceived idea of what to feel or experience. Since that time many books have been written on this subject, so an explanation or description is included with this 2nd Edition.

1. Body: The head should be erect and the spine straight. When you hold the SanTi posture your back should be straight.

2. Shoulders: The shoulders should be relaxed. In the common mistakes chapter you will see this. For beginners it is not easy to hold this posture and remained relaxed.

3. Arms: By keeping the arms slightly bent it allows the chi to flow. It also allows you to utilize the power. Too straight or bent will not allow a person to change quickly.

4. Hands: The power to both front and rear hands should be equal. In addition the rear hand helps to protect and add power to the front hand through the elbow energy points.

5. Fingers: They should firm to form the Hu Kou. As you gaze upon the index finger don't focus on it alone but see a 180 degree panorama.

6. Legs: Holding of the rear leg is the "rooting" of that leg to the earth. The front foot lightly touches the ground. This is a ready position.

7. Feet: Standing brings strength to the body, the toes should grip.

8. Hips: Tilt the hips forward to align with the spine.

9. Tongue: Curls and touches roof of mouth. Connects the

Dumo and Genmo meridians.

Health and Physical Fitness

H'sing-I is an internal style and, as we pointed out earlier, this system relies on soft natural movements. Even though softness is essential in the execution of the techniques, a well toned, strong body is also a requirement. Good exercise is necessary for good body conditioning. The obvious reason behind body conditioning is to improve one's health and ultimately lengthen one's life. The more immediate and practical reason however, is to increase one's endurance. In combat, for example, the person who cannot withstand the blows of his adversary will be defeated. Technique or only the knowledge of technique alone is not enough. The body is the tool through which the techniques are implemented. If a tool is rusty and in poor condition it is useless even to the greatest technician. Therefore, it is essential to keep the body in the best condition to achieve the best results from any technique. Pushups are a main source to begin to strengthen the hands. These are broken down into knuckle pushups, finger tip pushups, and tiger pushups. Strengthening exercises like these are always supplemented by stretching exercises. Flexibility is very important; the more flexible, the more freely the movements will be and the longer your lifespan. The tighter ones tendons are the shorter ones lifespan.

As pushups are self explanatory no pictures will be shown. (16)

(16) Since pushups are a very important part of our training and we do a unique style of them I have added them to the 2007 edition of the book.

Pushups

Here ShrFu Price's son demonstrates the proper push up form used in our Hsing-I system.

Fingertip pushups

Photo 17-1/2

Knuckle pushups

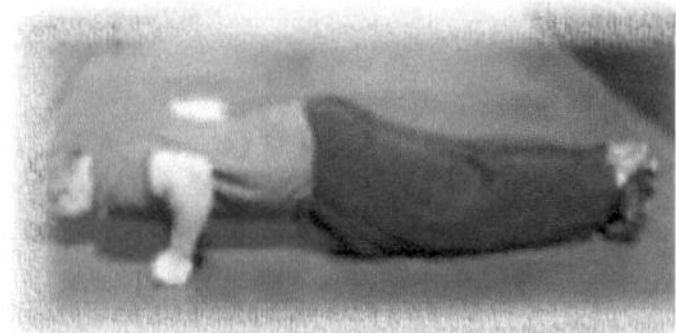

Photo 18-1

Our push ups were performed on Terrazzo floors. After 10 repetitions we would hold the position in photo 18-1 and rotate the whole body in a circular manner to build the wrist strength. We then would rise and continue to perform the push ups.

Stretching is a very important aspect of Kung Fu. Many books have given more than enough attention to this area, so we will only show one of our most useful exercises.

Start by taking either foot into your hand and stretch it out as far as possible.

(Photo 20-1) Repeat this 10 times and progressively stretch the leg higher and higher.

Photo 20-1

After ten repetitions, lower yourself down and back up to a standing position (Photos 20-1 and 20-2).

Photo 20-2

Many people who suffer from digestive problems, irregularity, greatly benefit themselves with the following exercise. In fact, Master Hsu told a story of an archeological dig in China that dug up writings and drawings showing this very exercise. The scrolls were dated over 2,000 years ago. Whether or not this is factual is not the point. The point is that it has been around a long time.

With the feet opened shoulder widths apart, raise the hands up to shoulder level. Snap them back as shown in (Photos 21-1 and 21-2) with 70% power. Raise arms to shoulder level again and repeat. The exercise is very simple and easy to execute. Repeat the action 50 times when you first start and gradually increase the repetitions until you can do 150.

Photo 21-1

Photo 21-2

This is not an instant cure all but after several months you will begin to feel a difference in your body. Perseverance is the key to results. This is true with all Kung Fu practice.

The three exercises in photos 22-1, 22-2and 22-3 are basic exercises for building lower abdominal strength.

As in photo 22-1, lay flat with toes curled upward. Inhale through your nose into the area of Tan Tien, hold the air. On the inhale raise your body up. Hold this for 5 seconds and then relax and exhale.

Photo 22-1

Take the same position as photo 22-2, only pull feet up by buttocks. Hands remain on kidneys. Inhale and hold breath as before. This time rise up on your toes. Hold for ten seconds and then relax and exhale as before.

Photo 22-2

This time put hands at your sides. Inhale, hold the air, and raise your legs and arms. Point the arms and fingers to the toes. (Photo 22-3) Hold for ten seconds and then relax.

Photo 22-3

Do these three every morning, and after a few months you will become stronger and have more stomach strength.

THE INTERNAL

The Internal is a subject that is discussed by everyone who practices Kung Fu.

The Internal or Nei Kung as opposed to the external (Wei Kung) is inside power. This power you cannot see. It comes from the inside of your body. Wei Kung is muscle power and anybody can see this kind of power.

To develop your Nei Kung requires daily practice. It is not a visible change or instant change, but takes a great deal of time. When your practice is good, your internal organs will be free from stress and your health will improve.

The following exercise will help to build your Nei Kung. These are used daily by all of Master Hsu's students with good results.

Tiger Playing with Ball

Begin the exercise with the right hand and forearm parallel to the ground at the throat level. The left hand and arm are parallel at the navel (Photo 23-1).

Photo 23-1

Inhale through the nose; begin twisting to the left and exhale. (Photo 23-1)

Photo 23-2

Change hands and inhale. Twist slowly to the right and exhale (Photo 23-3). This exhale should last the duration of the twist. Change hands and inhale through the nose again. Twist to the left and exhale. This should be repeated 10 times.

Photo 23-3

The next exercise in this series is very good to stretch the abdominal muscles and chest. It improves the circulation of blood and Chi and generally relaxes the body. Begin by opening the legs slightly wider than the shoulders. The hands are at navel height (Photo 24-1).

Photo 24-1

Inhale through your nose into the Tan Tien (3" below navel) while inhaling the right palm moves downward and to the rear. (Photo 24-2)

Slightly turn your upper torso to the left as your eyes watch the right heel. Hold this position for several seconds. Relax and exhale simultaneously. The hands come back to the original position.

Photo 24-2

Repeat this exercise now going in the opposite direction. (Photo 24-3)

Photo 24-3

The final exercise begins as before with the feet slightly wider than the shoulders. Raise the arms until they reach the shoulders. Bend the arm inward until they form a circle. Drop the hands downward, relaxing as you form the position. The eyes stare between the two hands, focusing them on the tip of the nose. (Photo 25) Now close your eyes as if in meditation. Quietly stand in this position until it becomes unbearable and the legs begin to shake then relax. Increase the length of time as much as you can everyday.

Photo 25

Progress here is not easy to see. Be patient and set aside a time everyday to do this and you will slowly feel the change in your body. The exercises presented here are only a few of the many exercises that are part of Kung Fu. They have been proven by countless generations of Kung Fu practitioners.

As mentioned before, Kung Fu encompasses more than mere physical exercise. In order to truly study you must study the yin aspect of Kung Fu. The yin is something you cannot see. Included in this section is "Nei Kung," of course, but seldom does anyone realize that a complete Kung Fu teacher must be able to treat external as well as internal maladies, and for this very reason Kung Fu has been said to require decades to learn. Learning to fight and break someone is very easy to learn. After a few years you con become proficient. To learn to diagnose a kidney infection, fire in the liver, bladder or spleen problem is not as simple to learn as a down block. Broken arms and fingers cannot be left bent and crooked because of lack of practice in setting them. I do not think a person would have very many students if every problem was compounded when the teacher touched it.

So by necessity it takes a long time to learn these things. When I studied setting a bone in the forearm, I first watched Shoufu Hsu. The next time I placed my hands on his and could feel the bones set in place.

After several times, I tried with guidance from my teacher to set the bone. Any mistake was covered by him.

Now, a broken arm is not an everyday occurrence, so this process is indeed lengthy.

Learning to look at a person's face to see what is wrong on the inside of his body is even more difficult to learn. Here though, charts and notes can be made to help later in diagnosis.

After a diagnosis has been made, treatment is necessary. Here the Chinese have basically four methods: acupuncture, moxabustion, acupressure, and herbs.

Acupuncture is the fastest method of the three. It will either increase or decrease the flow of Chi in the body. Moxa and acupressure are next in that order. To heal completely though requires the use of herbs in conjunction with the above techniques.

In the following (Photos 26-1 and 26-2) a Moxa point for men only is demonstrated. This point is known as the "San Li" point. It helps to stimulate your energy and improve your circulation. When using this point, burn six cones on the point. When burning the cone, endure the heat but don't burn yourself. Repeat everyday until you feel the difference. Very seldom does a one day effect take place.

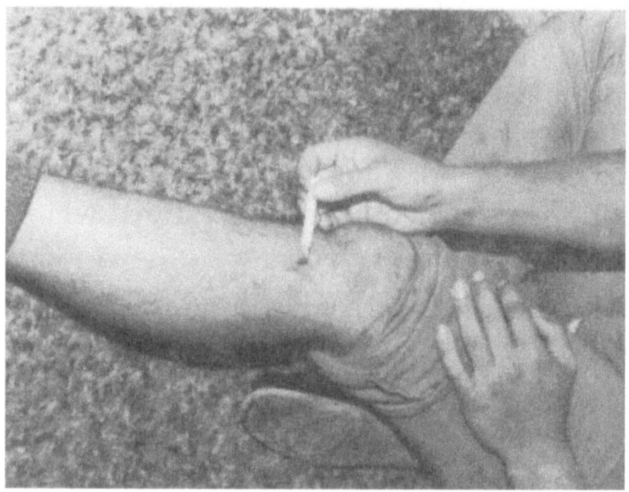

Photo 26-1

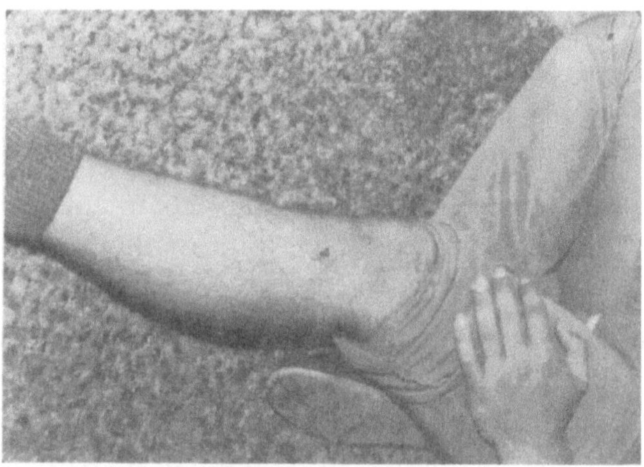

Photo 26-2

Our next points will probably receive appreciation by many people. The two points in (Photo 27-1 and 27-2) are for relieving lower back pain. As before, burn at least six cones on each side of the spine. Chronic back pains often require herbs along with the Moxa.

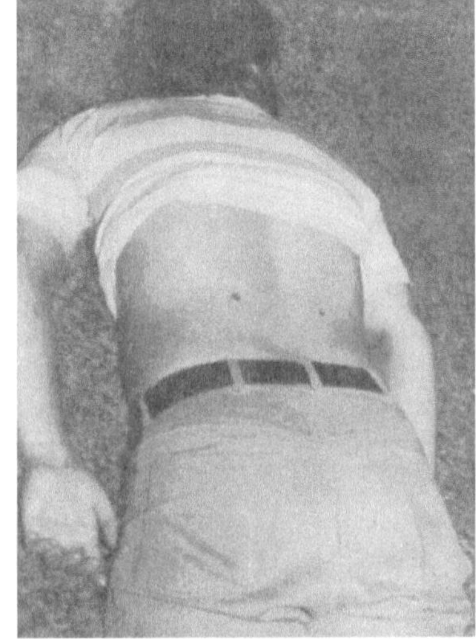

Photo 27-1

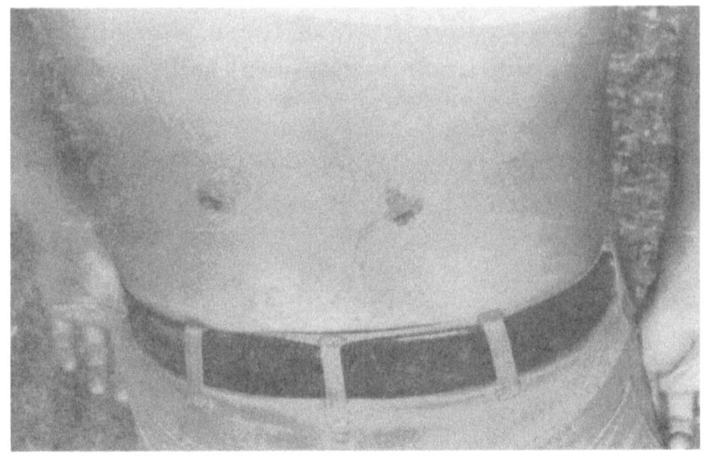

Photo 27-2

Acupressure is the use of pressure on the meridian points. This can be applied by thumbs, fingers, palms and even your elbows. In reality you can use acupressure on any point on the body. As this book is not solely for the purpose of healing, we only show two techniques.

In photo 28 the palms are used to apply an even steady pressure down the spine. Too much pressure should always be avoided. Do the entire spine from shoulders to tailbone and repeat as often as you like.

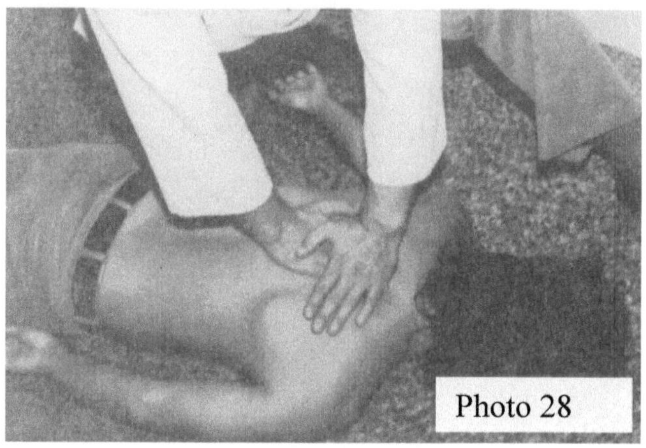
Photo 28

In photo 29 the index fingers and thumbs give a more concentrated pressure along the sides of the spine. As before repeat as often as you like. Both of these techniques stimulate chi to flow up the spine and for a general feeling of well being.

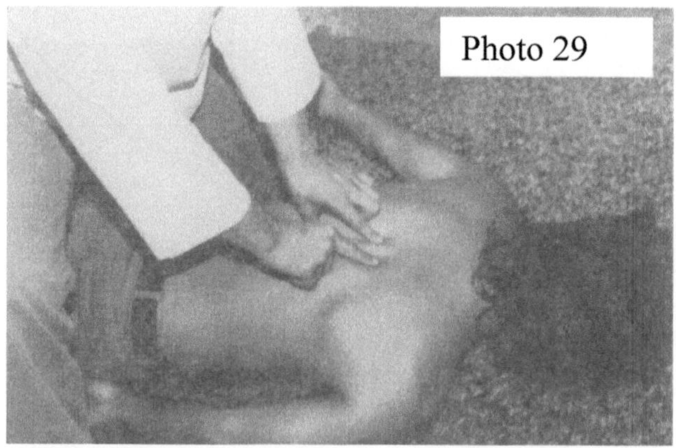
Photo 29

Photos 30 and 31 demonstrate techniques for setting bones. The hands are very easily broken and in the Martial Arts this happens quite often. The setting appears easy enough but the thing you can't see in these pictures is the feeling it takes to know when it is right. A lengthy description would be useless to anyone without proper guidance in even these basic setting techniques.

In photo 30 the forefinger is being set by a steady pull. Practice is necessary of course. In photo 31, the thumb is set using the same pulling motion.

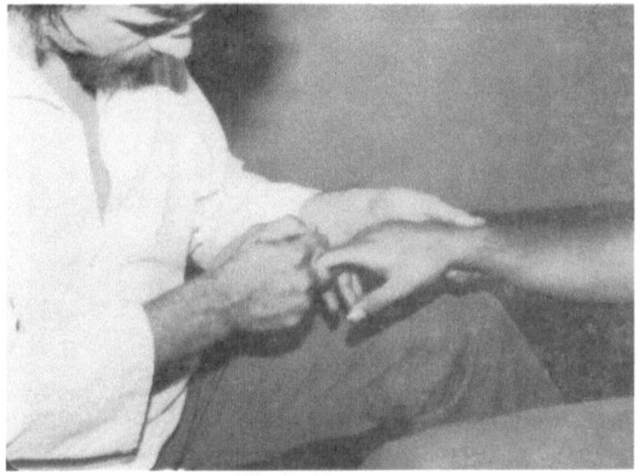

Photo 30

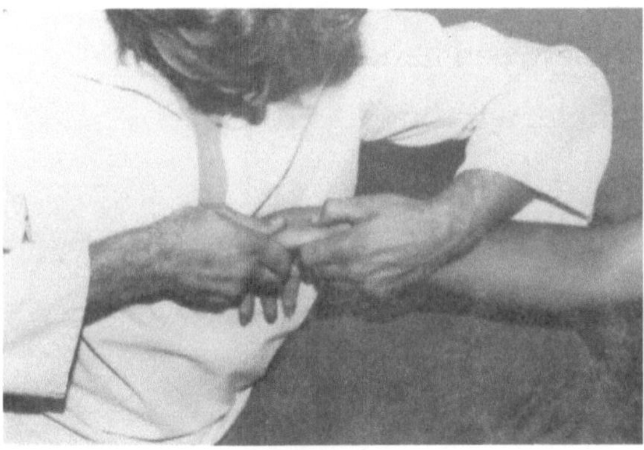

Photo 31

In conclusion, on healing let me say this, "it is truly the hardest part to learn." Extreme patience and practice is the way to have your teacher show you.

Not being a publication on Shaolin, Master Hsu agreed nonetheless to include a section on the Shaolin Hand Techniques and governing principles.

18 HAND TECHNIQUES

1. Shuin--to follow
2. Men--to feel with hand, to hold
3. Tih--to raise by hand or lift
4. An--to press or control with hand
5. Tan--To rebound
6. Nien--To twist with fingers
7. Tsuo--To rub between hands
8. Pan--To entangle, winding
9. Tuei--Push
10. Nei--Contain
11. Dong--Move
12. Eao--To wave, shake away
13. Chuo--Claw, nail
14. Che--To cut
15. Jin--To advance
16. Tuei--To retreat, withdraw
17. Chu--Appear, overtake, escape, come out
18. Shir--To take in, to absorb

Shaolin, like the Taoist styles, copied animals for its fighting attitudes and principles. This simply means that the actions of the body perform according to actions taken from the animal that influenced the action of the movement.

The following six conditions apply to the Shaolin Techniques:

1. Cat twist
2. Dog chase
3. Freezing chicken steps
4. Eagle eyes
5. Monkey hands
6. Fox heart

The body construction is said to be according to the following:

1. Cubic--Bulky as the ocean.
2. Spherical--Round as floating ball.
3. Angular--Sharp as rolling stone.

When the body actions are good the hand actions must be learned. Of all the techniques there are the 18 Hand Techniques which were previously listed.

In the Shaolin Styles, which are Buddhist, the first 5 degrees coincide with the 5 Chan of Buddhism.

The 5 Chan are as follows:

1. External Tao
2. Human
3. Monk
4. Buddha
5. Supreme lotus seat

"Chi"- The Magnificent Chi:

Gentleness

Tolerance

Loyalty

Potential

However diversified the art of Kung Fu may be, the utmost spirit is unique and uniform.

KUNG FU originated for "Nature"

Nature →→→ ←←←Against Nature

Emptiest→ Empty→ Spirit→ Chi→ Vigor→ Shape→ Movement

Sit Chen ↔ Soft Ch'uan ↔ Hard Ch'uan

Sit Pi Ch'uan

HUMAN LIFE: Step (1) plus (2) forms a cycle.

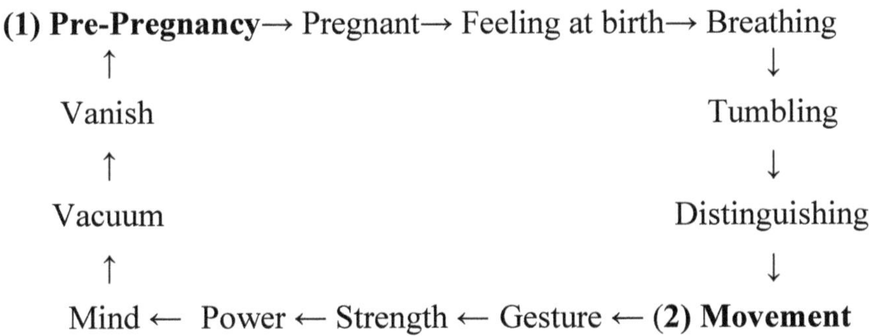

Sit Chen is somewhat like meditation but brings one to a condition that "I am no where everywhere I can be."
The Soft Ch'uan is the utmost a normal person can reach.

Illness or trouble	**Treatment**
1. Bruises	Tieh Ta Yao*
2. Dislocation or Breaks	Herbal Poultice and setting technique.
3. Sprains	Set bones and Tieh Ta Yao*
4. Swollen Muscles	Poultice for muscle**
5. Rheumatism	Tieh Ta Yao* and A.M. ***
6. Arthritis	Moxa and herbs
7. Intestinal Disorder	A.M. *** and herbs
8. Hemorrhoids	Herbs
9. Concussions	Herbs
10. Back Pains	Moxa, A.M. *** and herbs
11. Sciatica	A.M. ***
12. Insomnia	A.M. ***

A cure cannot be claimed on the before mentioned ailments, although great improvement is quite often affected. The Chinese place immense faith in these treatments. Of the students aided by these herbs, no complaints have arisen.

*Tieh Ta Yao- Liniment prepared with herbs and whiskey for external use only. **Special poultice for injuries caused by being struck on the muscle. ***A.M. - Acupressure Massage

2007 2nd Edition

This medicinal portion of the Manual is very rudimentary. Very few teachers and hardly any practitioners even knew that bone setting, acupressure, moxa and meditation were part of the original Chinese Martial Arts. When Master Hsu came here he decided to make a publication that would explain to the American public just how deep the Chinese Martial Arts are. Even today as I search the Internet I read comments by people who haven't the slightest idea what a true martial art is all about. There is much more than just punching and kicking.

In the present day and age, some of the things that are learned in the Tang Shou Tao would be a liability if practiced. Bone setting is a good example. When my middle son fell at school and broke his collar bone he was sent to a doctor where the bone was set. The very next day he fell and dislodged the bone. I set the bone and applied an herbal poultice to help it mend. I would never do that to anyone now outside of my family. The liability would be tremendous.

International Tang Shou Tao Association Members

(1977)

The International Tang Shou Tao Association was formed with a charter and officers elected on 7-7-77. Master Hsu was of course the President elect, with ShrFu John Price as Vice-President, Janet Price secretary and Morris Hadley as Treasurer.

ShrFu Price receiving Certificate

Master Hsu, Sifu Wong Morris Hadley, Janet Price

Mike Bingo

Master Hsu and John Price

Dale Shigenaga

The two top pictures were taken at the formation of the Tang Shou Tao Association. John Price, Dale Shigenaga and Mike Bingo are a few of the original members still teaching and spreading the teachings of Master Hsu.

Herbal Recipes

The following herbs are for external use only. No cure is claimed. People should use them only after they have been diagnosed as needing them. Neither the Author nor the publisher takes any responsibility for their misuse.

1. Muscle Powders (Chinese Ice)

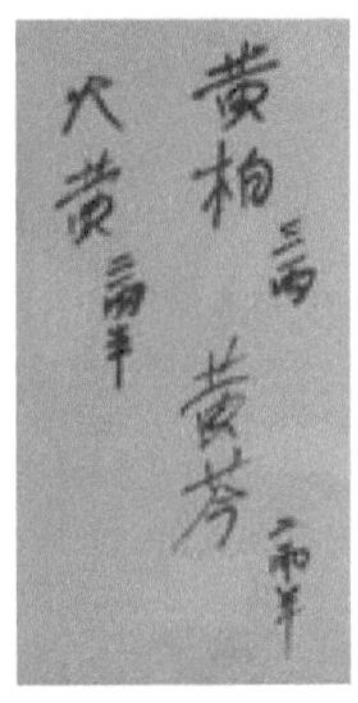

This is a classic herbal formula for the martial artist, it can also be used for sports injuries or riding your bicycle. The compound is for all sorts of muscle injuries. Any sort of trauma to the muscle, to include small strains and tears, has been treated with this powder.

The herbs must be ground to a fine powder form and then mixed with egg whites. The powder must be the consistency of whipped butter.

Apply the mixture to the affected area and cover with gauze. Then top that with a plastic to allow it to be sealed with tape. Leave on for 24 hours then change. Use for three days and then rest a day before using again. If a rash appears, discontinue until the rash is gone.

2. Arthritis

The following recipe again is for external use only.

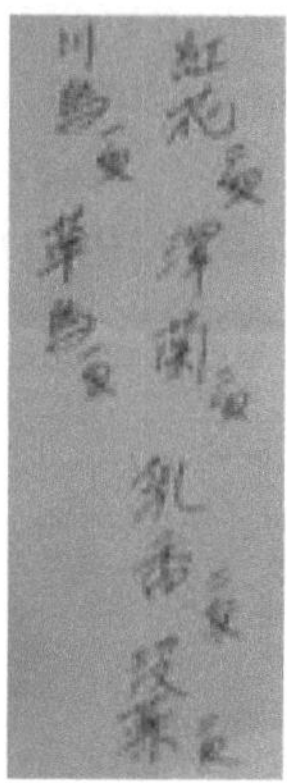

This recipe is for arthritis or rheumatism not rheumatoid arthritis. It can be used in conjunction with Tieh Ta Jaow.

Mix this recipe with two slices of crushed ginger and add to 3 cups of water. Gently simmer until there are 2 cups remaining. Massage the affected area with a cloth soaked in the mixture. You can use the brew for approximately 5 times and then it will need to be changed.

For any questions about these or any of our other recipes you can contact us at our web site www.jlprice.clearwire.net

If, you cannot obtain the herbs please contact us through the web site. We can provide them in the raw form or powdered.

Epilog

When I was first approached about republishing the Masters' Manual, I was asked to add a section detailing or explaining what I had learned since the first edition was published in 1977.

What I have learned was already in the book or passed to me through oral transmission. Most important of all is to practice. Even if you don't practice H'sing-I for a martial application, the exercise is very, very beneficial. It is the single most useful thing that you can do for yourself regarding health. Bulk muscle is not as important as good toned muscle and flexibility. Death is aligned with stiffness and rigidity. Life is aligned with movement and flexibility. Compare the vibrant willow tree versus the dead tree with its brittle branches and you know exactly what I am talking about.

Good balance is a necessity in all aspects of our lives. H'sing-I is about balance, not only in martial application, but also in our daily lives. It is a way of life. Oh, there are other styles and programs that say the same thing and they probably also work, but I chose H'sing-I. My whole life has been based on the guidelines that I learned from my teachers. In everyday life, it is far better to bend a little rather than hit every problem head on. The road is quite often rough and filled with boulders; sidestepping these is better than bumping into them. This is not to say that with H'sing-I you won't have problems. You will just be able to deal with them easier. Keeping your balance also refers to your emotional stability. I have learned not to get too giddy or over-joyous about my good tidings or get too depressed about any bad news. A circle represents the Tai Chi Tui. Good and bad, in all of their degrees, always roll around. That is why when something not so good happens, I can smile because the good balance will be coming my way as sure as day follows night.

The next important thing that I have learned to recognize is change. In the martial arts the person who can change the smoothest and quickest will probably win. The same attitude or philosophy applies to your daily life. I have an electrical contracting business. Quite often a field supervisor will ask me why I changed my schedule in the middle of the day. An emergency power outage in someone's home changes my priorities. This and other instances affect our lives on a daily basis. We need to be able to change to cope with it.

These are the most important things that I have learned from my 41 plus years studying the martial arts. I still enjoy the practice and the contact, but I no longer feel the need to compete with anything or anyone.

www.ingramcontent.com/pod-product-compliance
Ingram Content Group UK Ltd.
Pitfield, Milton Keynes, MK11 3LW, UK
UKHW041924190726
13854UKWH00003B/1423